Madalas
Adult Coloring Book

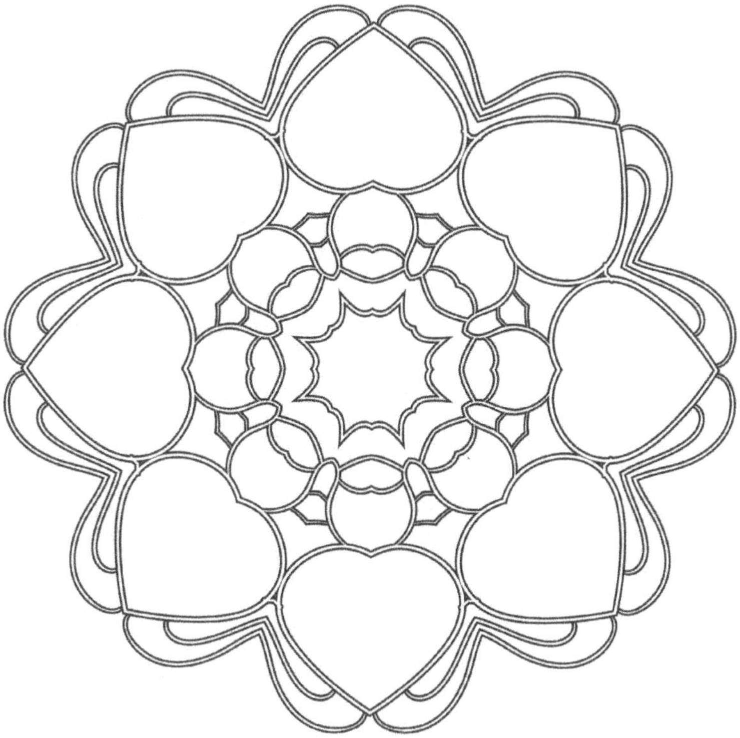

Belinda L. Frazier

Madalas
Adult Coloring Book

Published June 2016

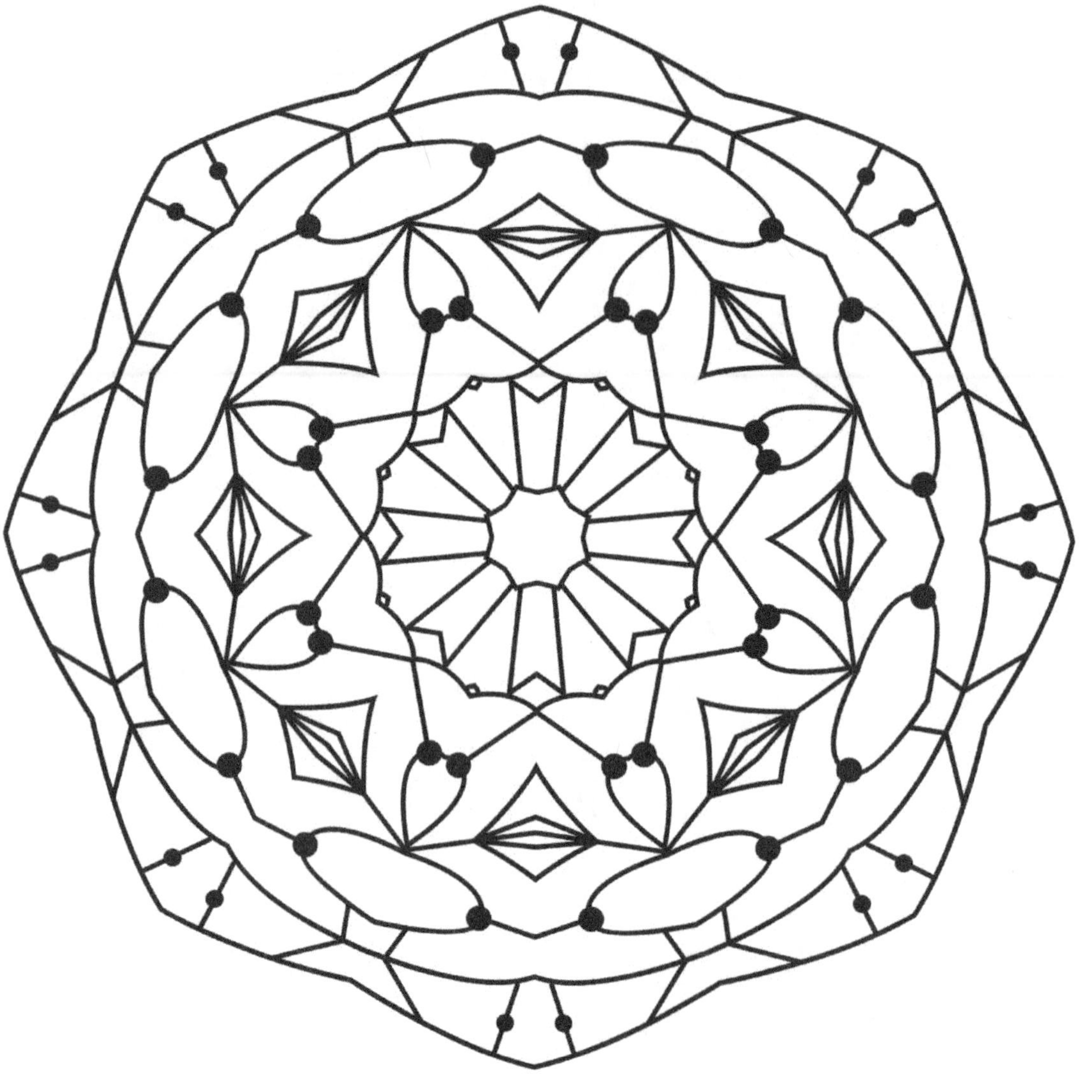

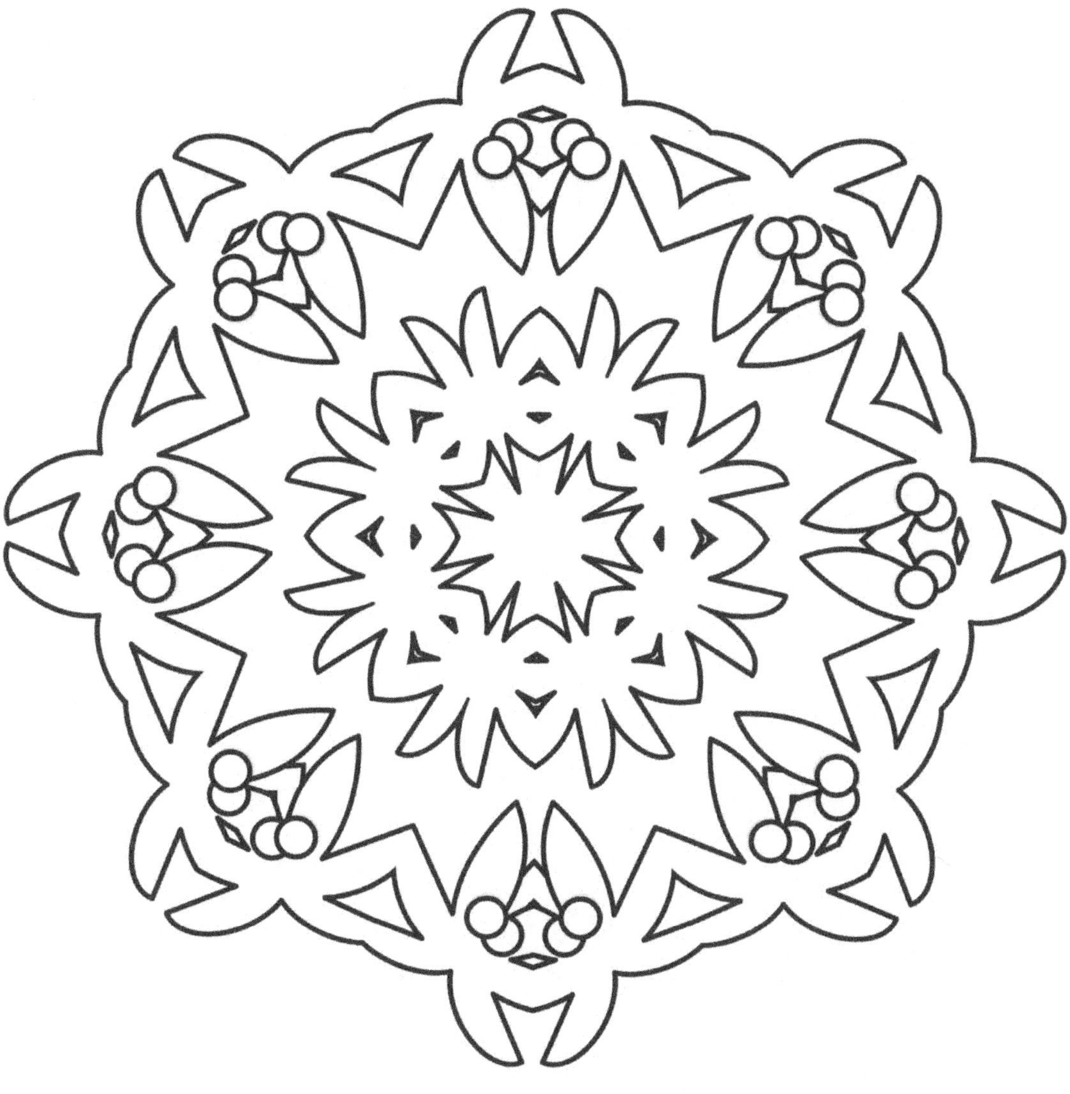

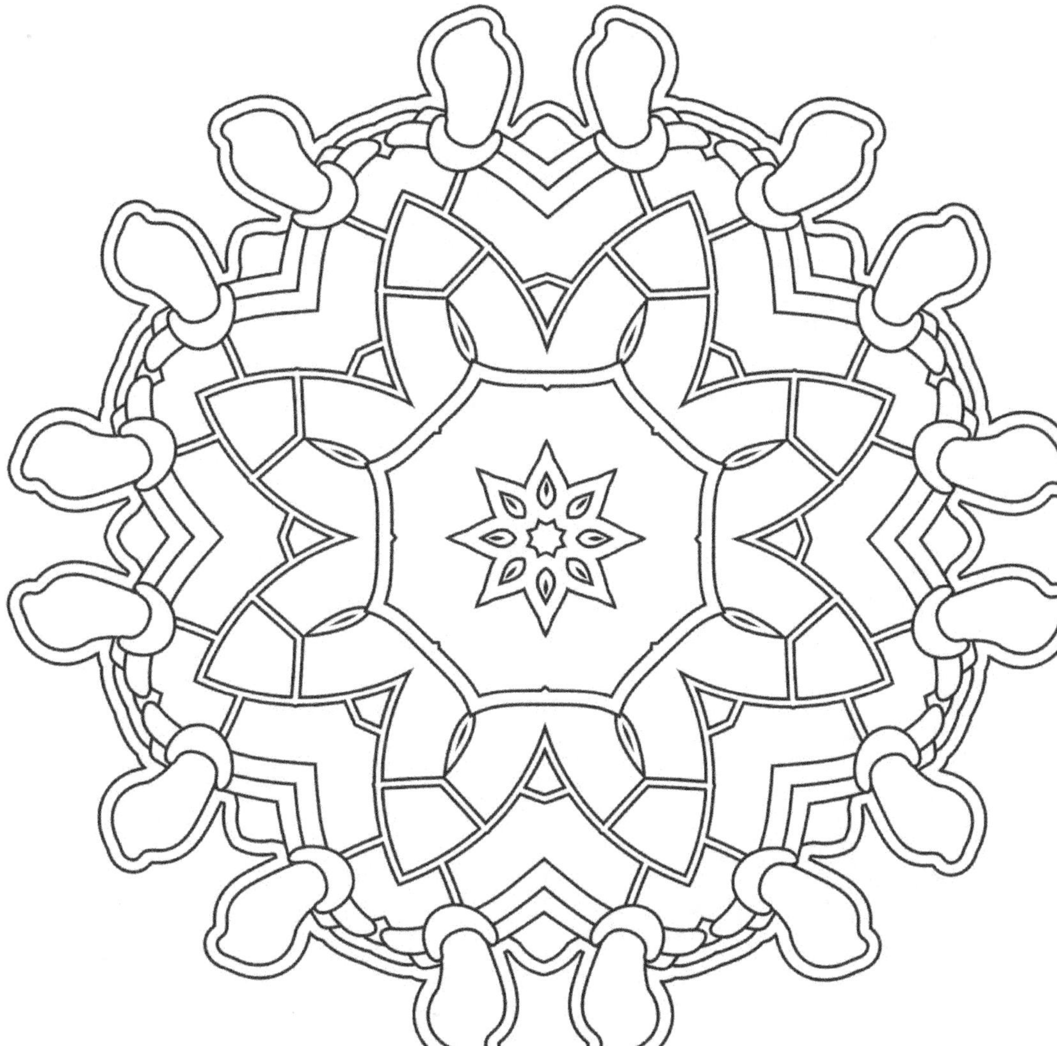

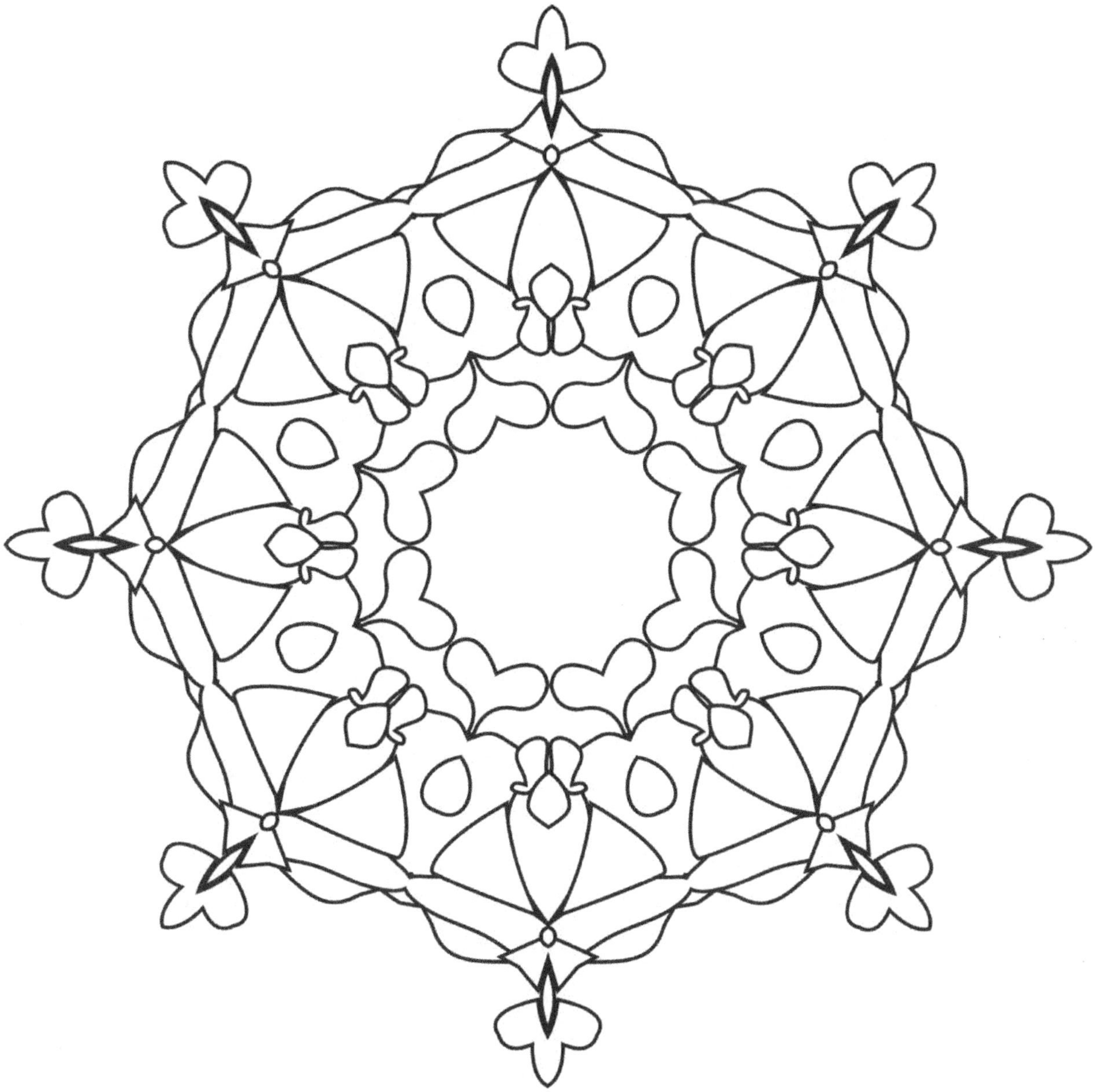

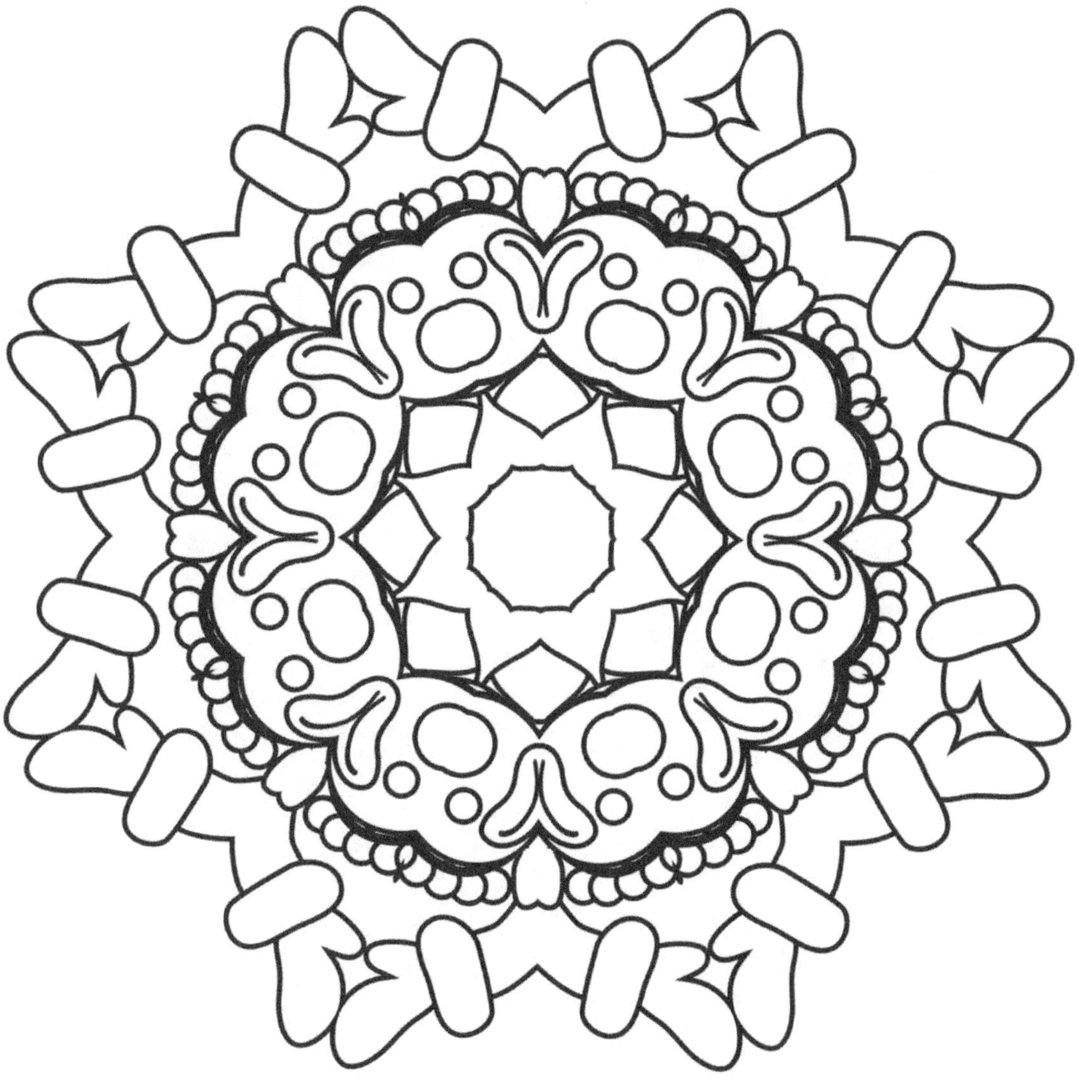

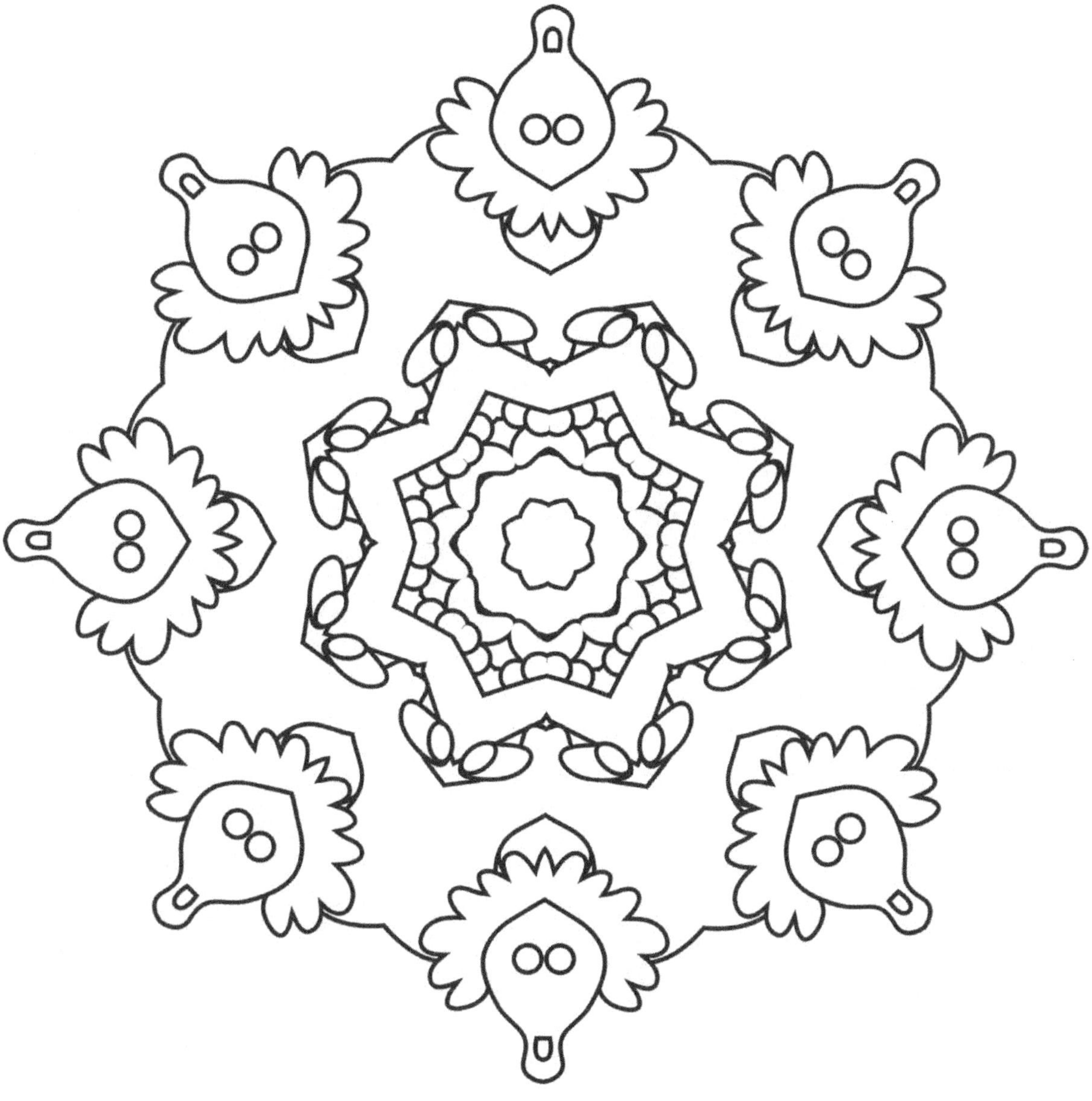

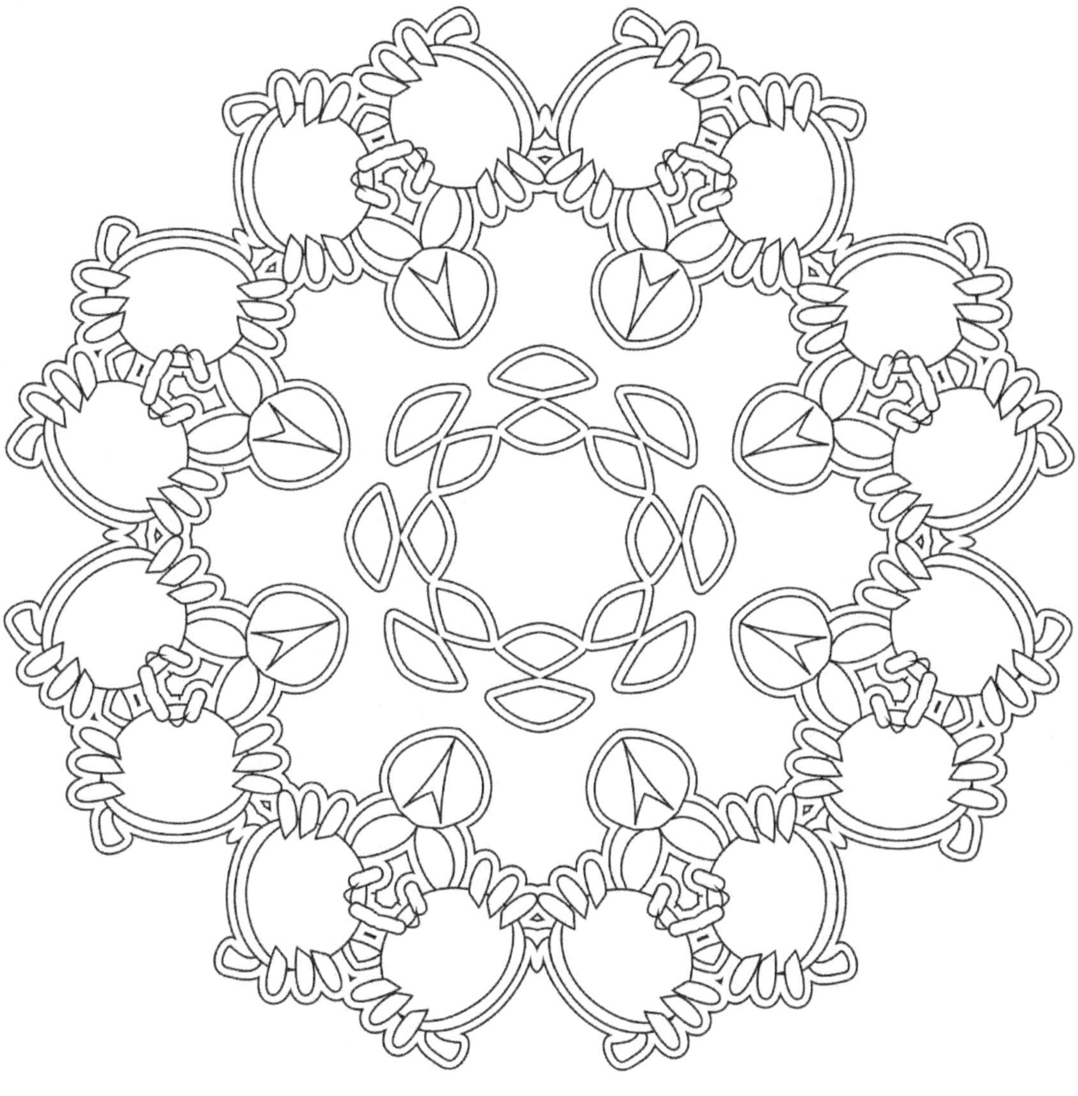

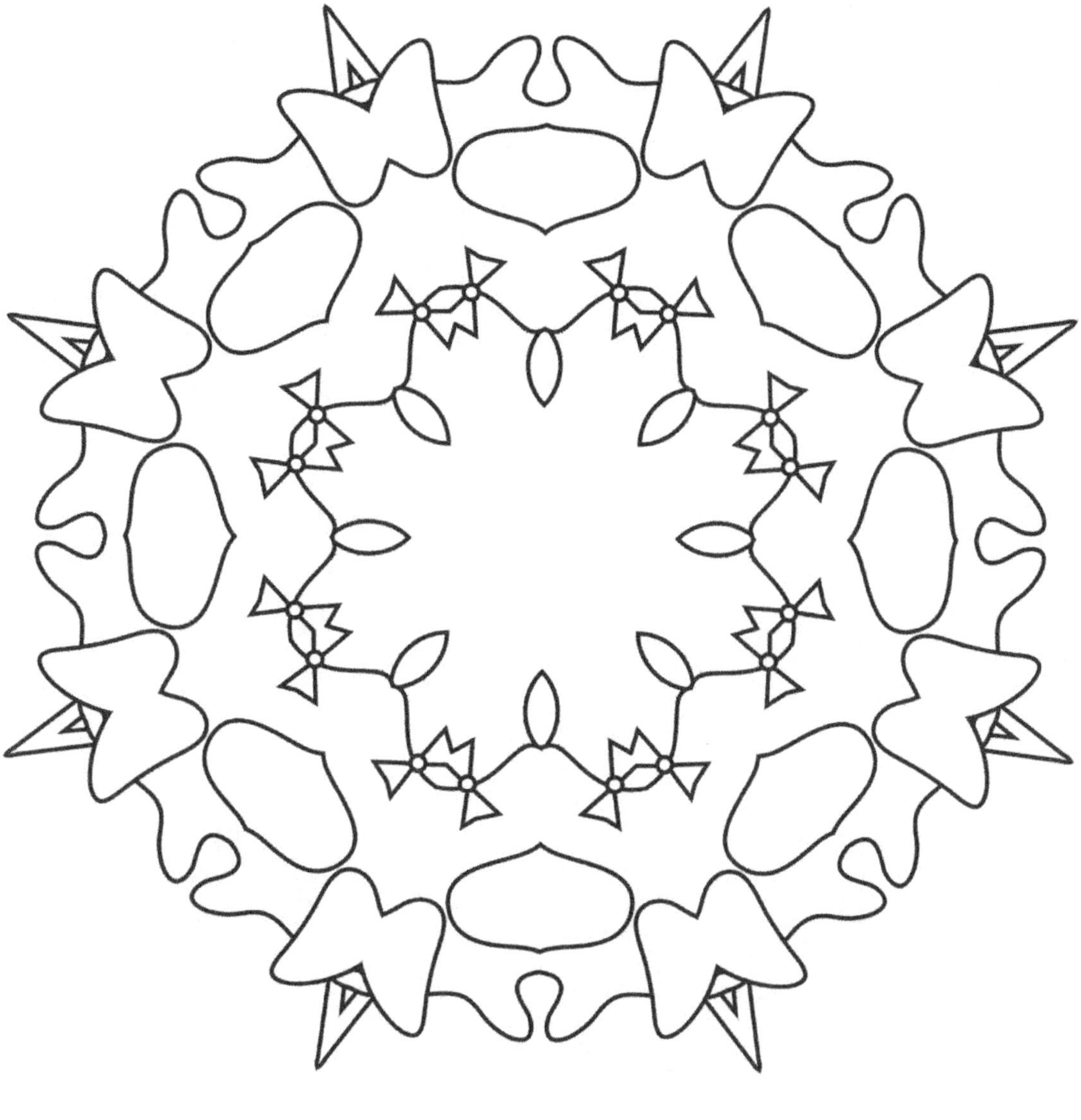

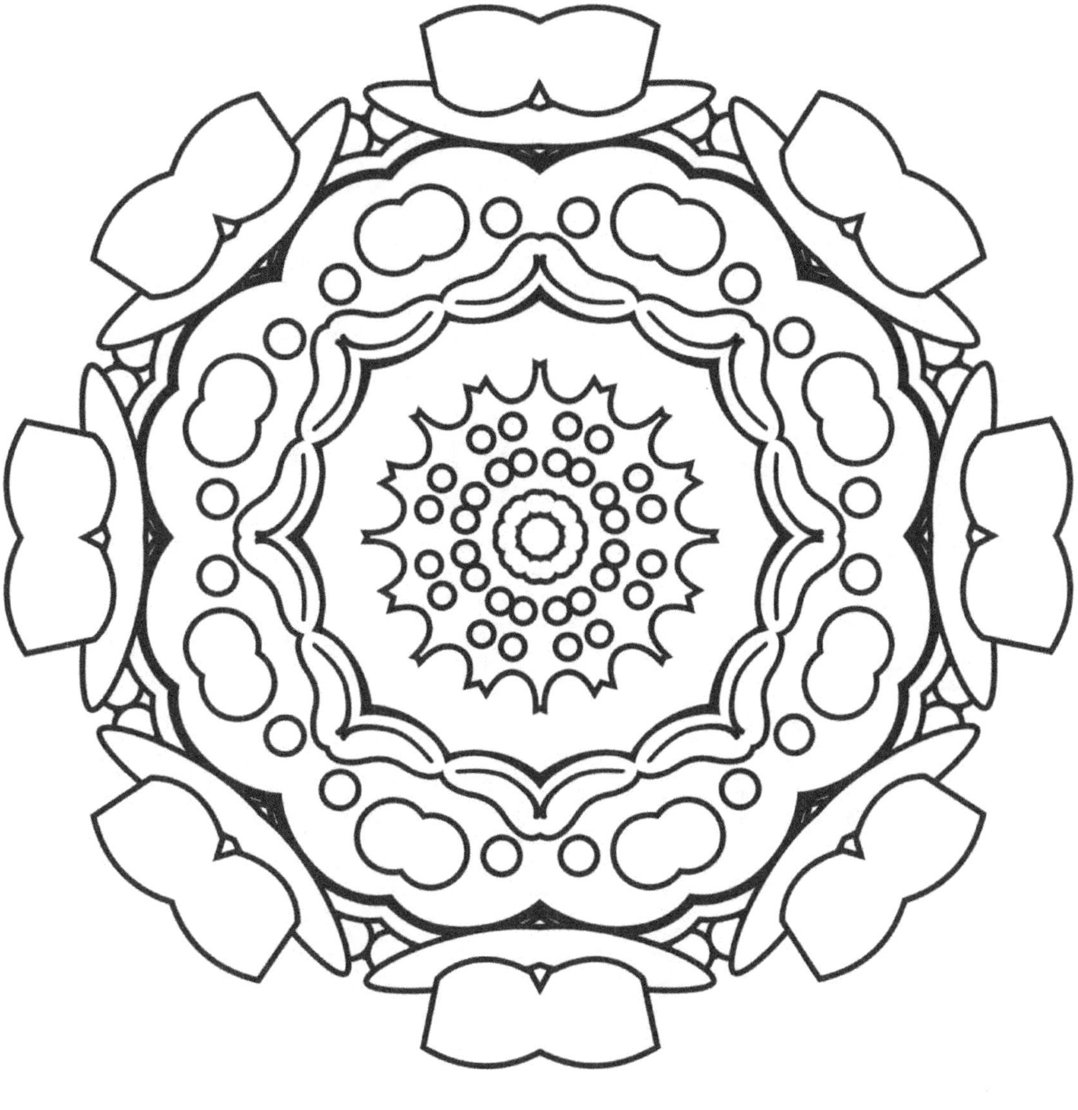

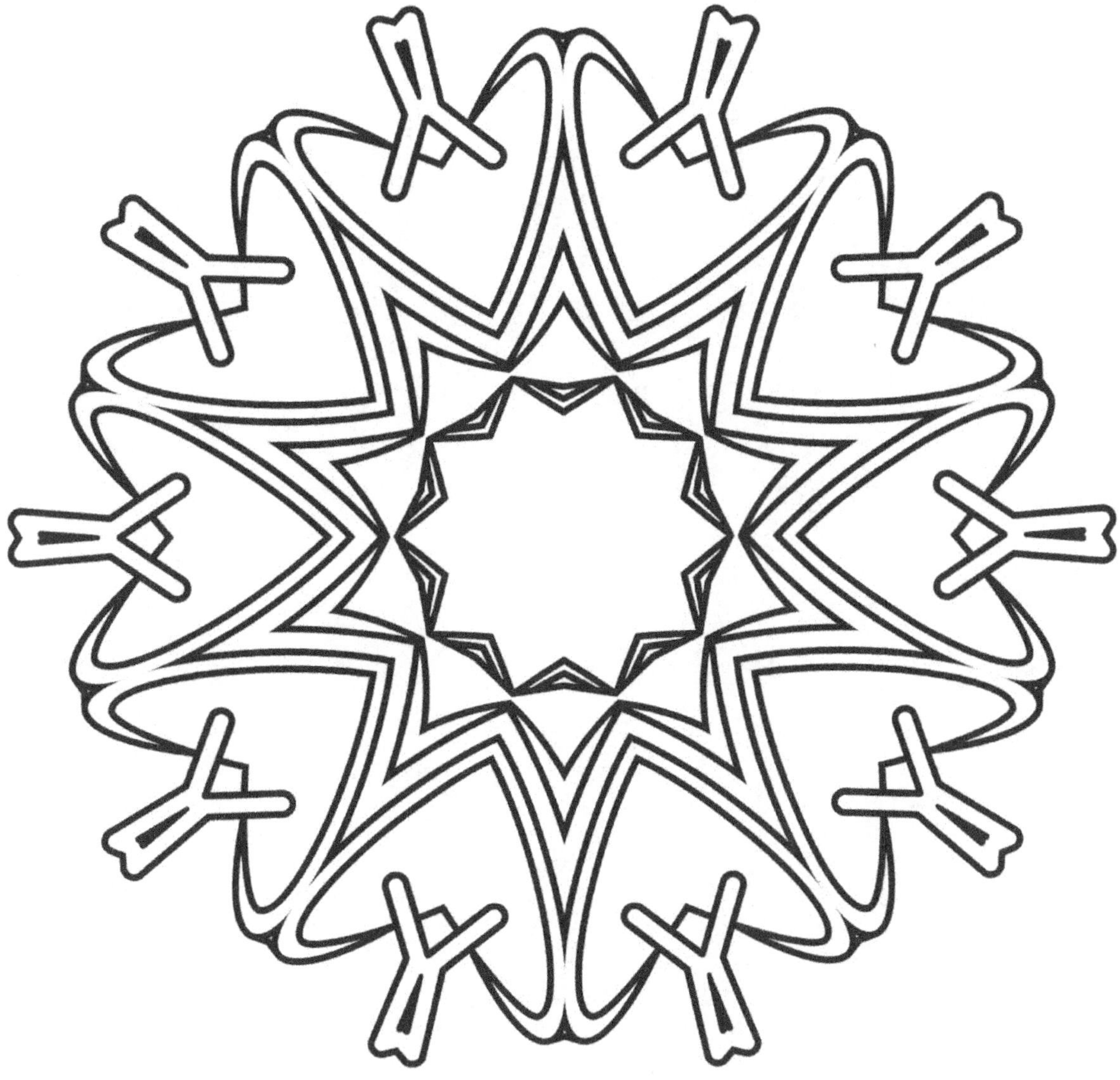

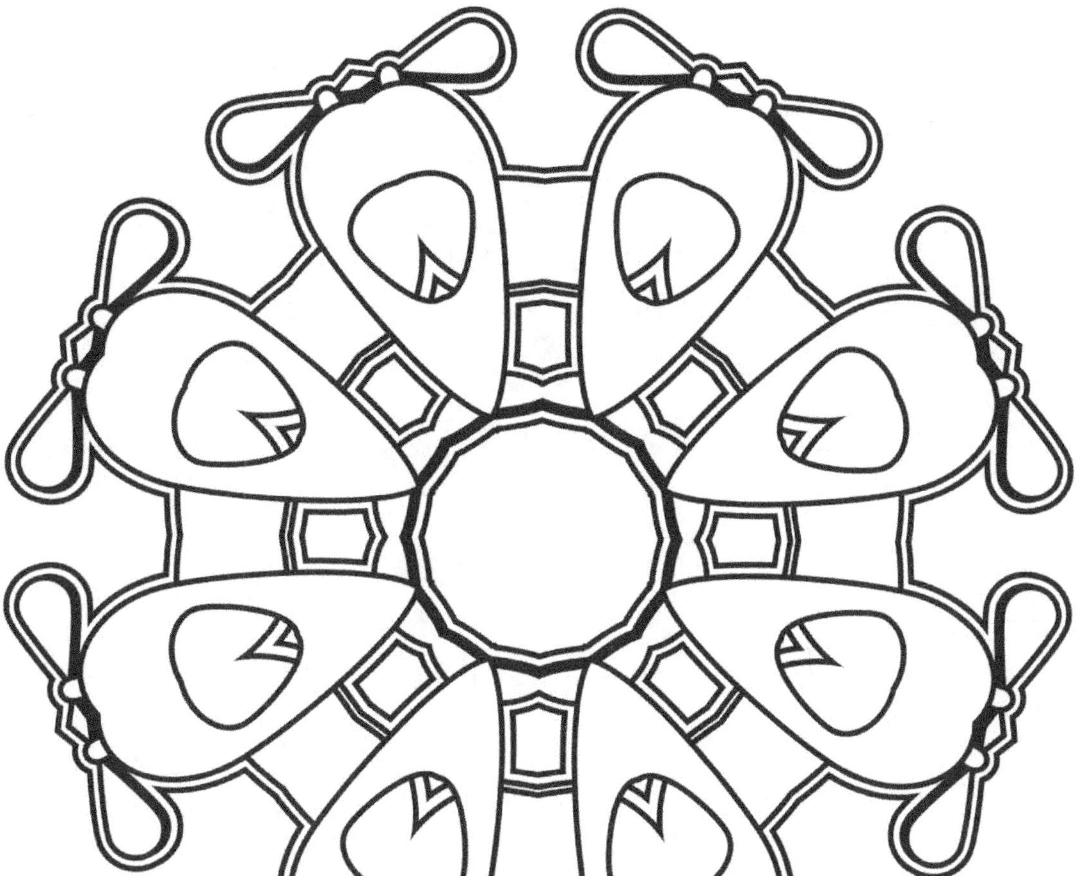

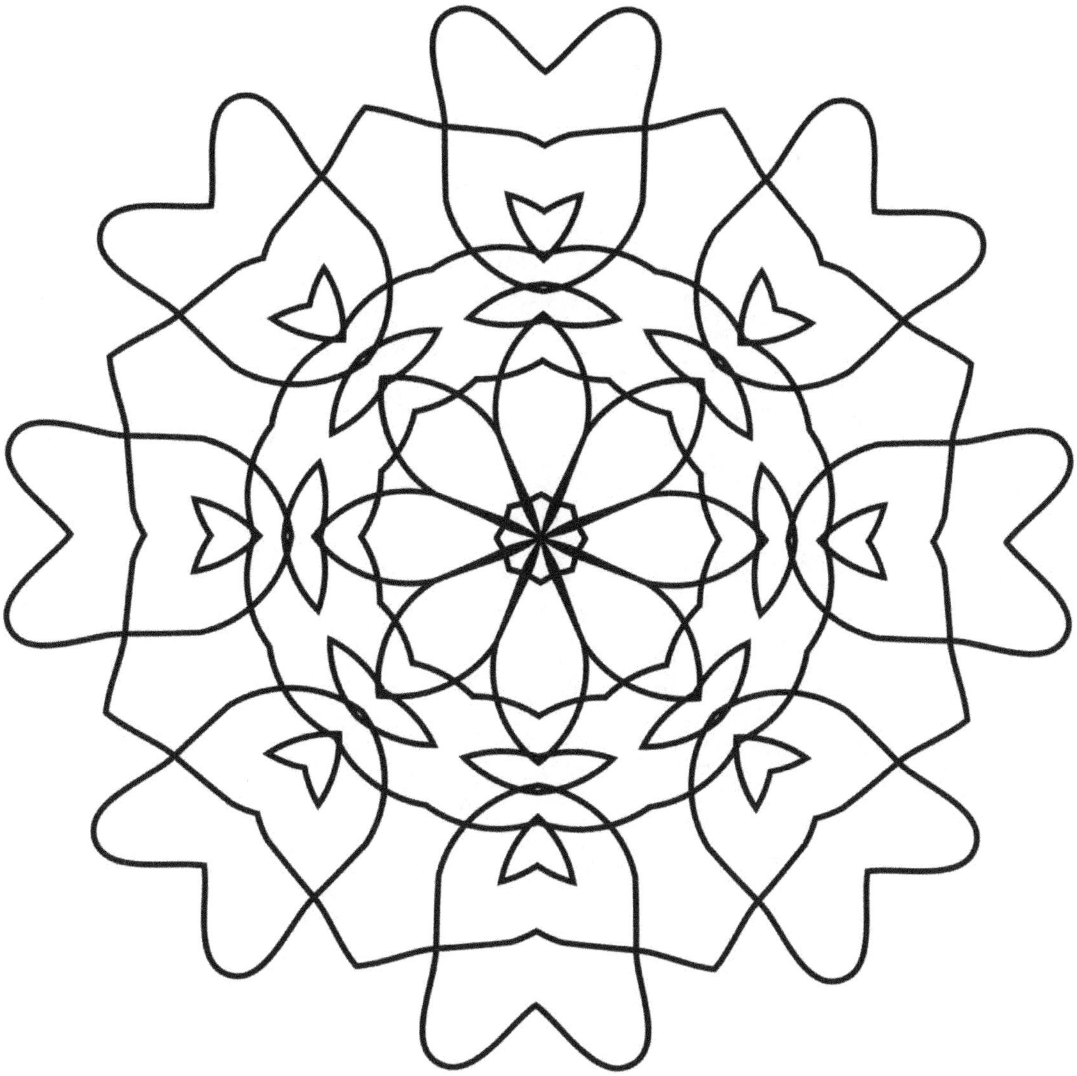

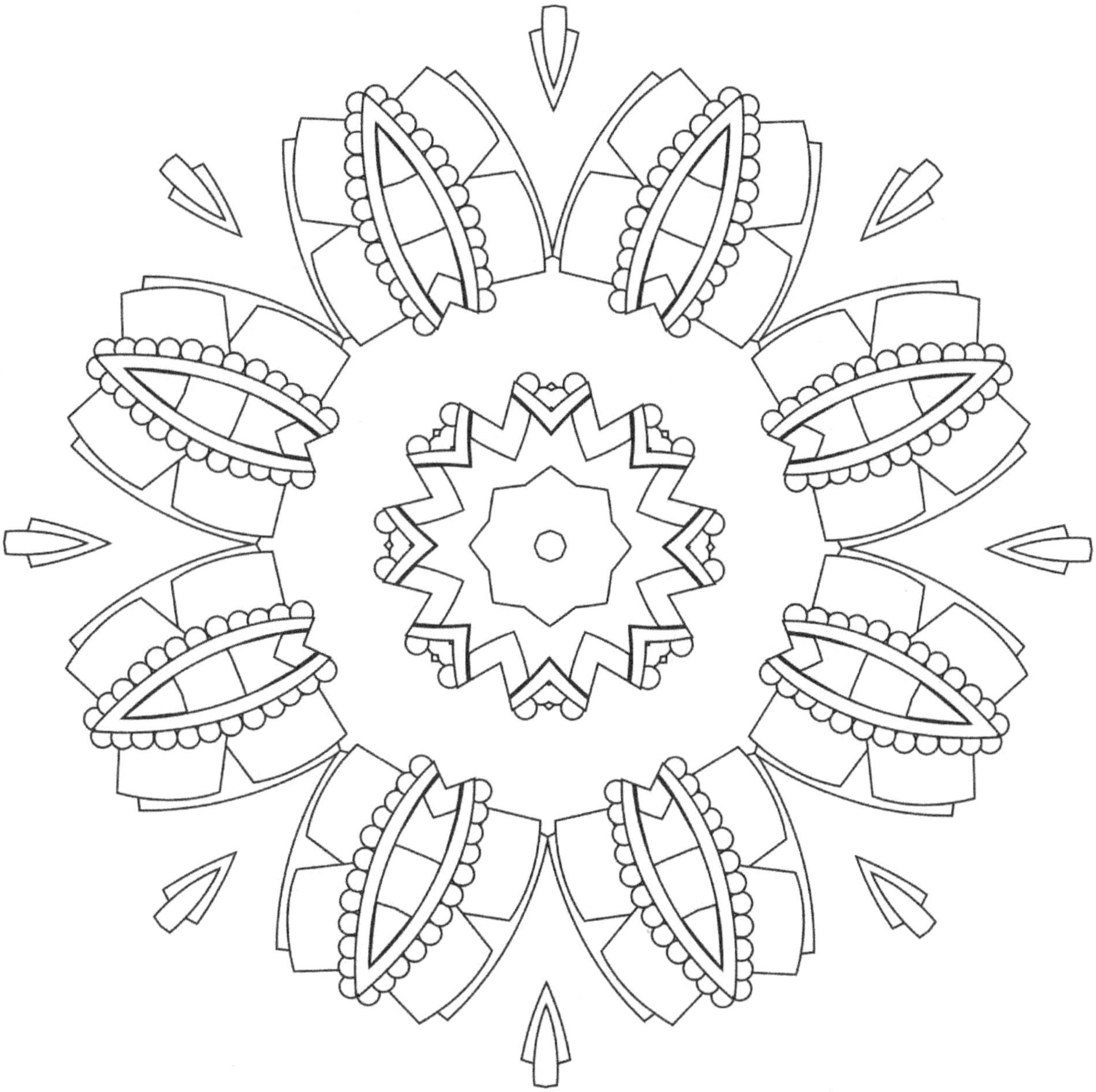

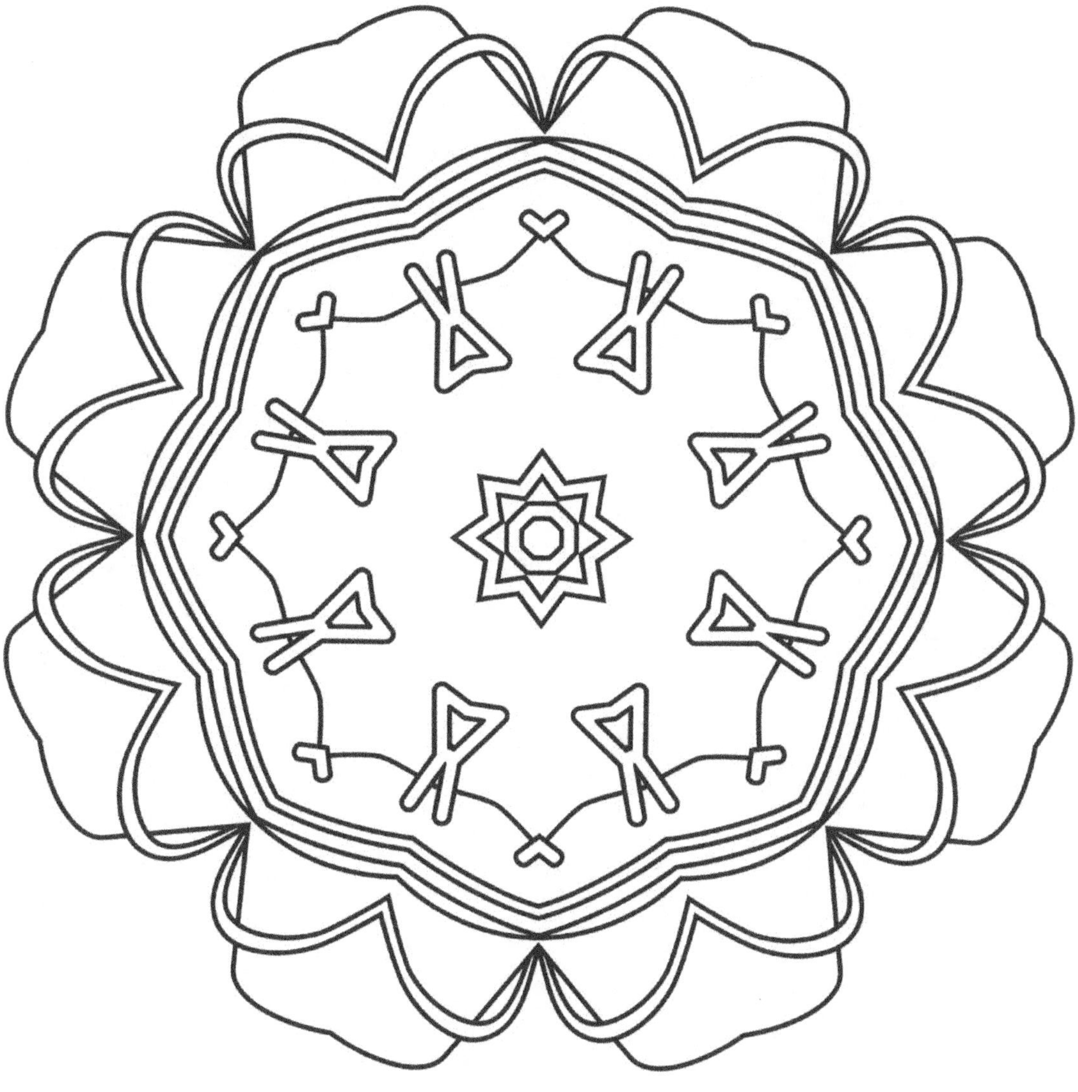

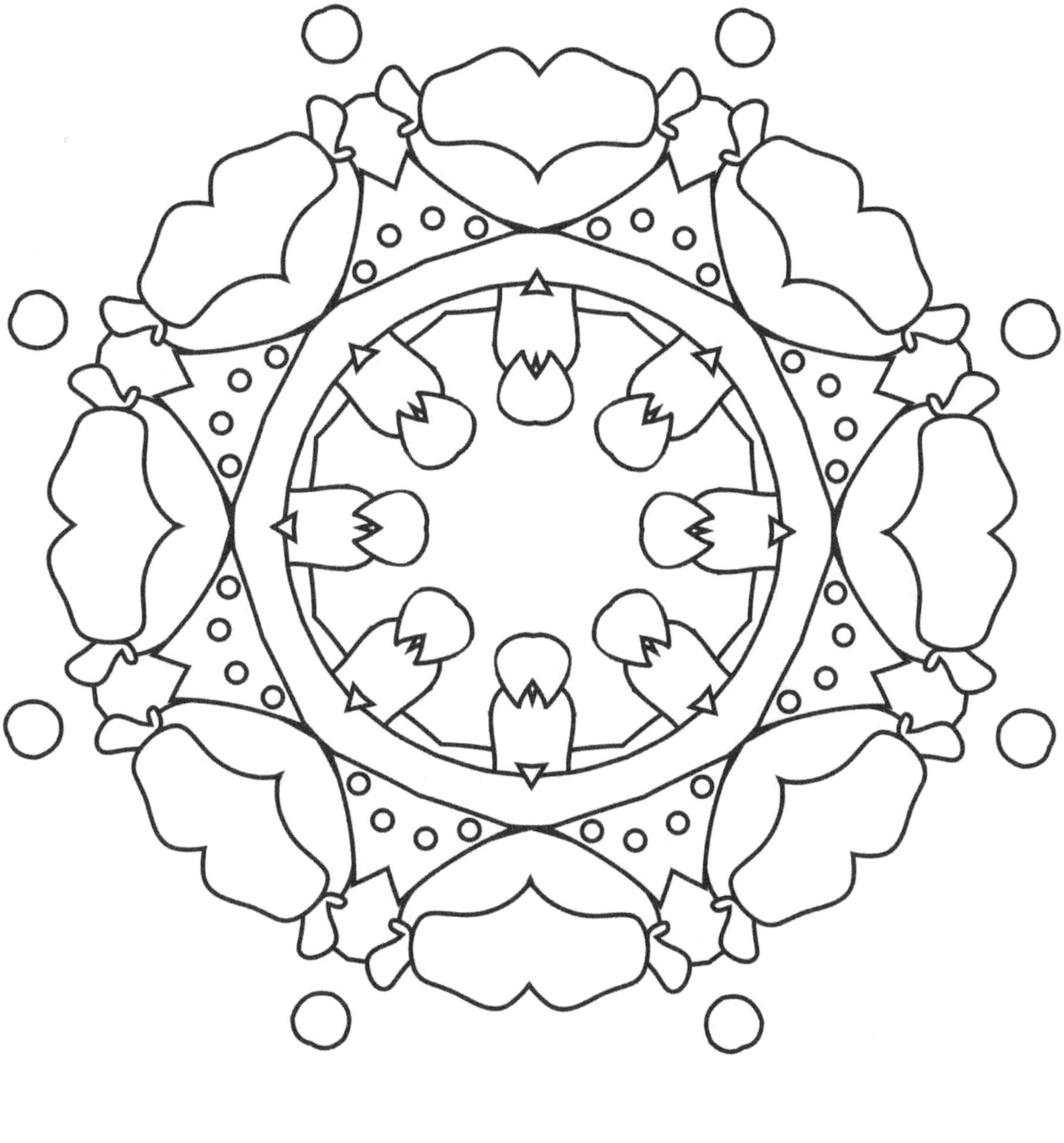

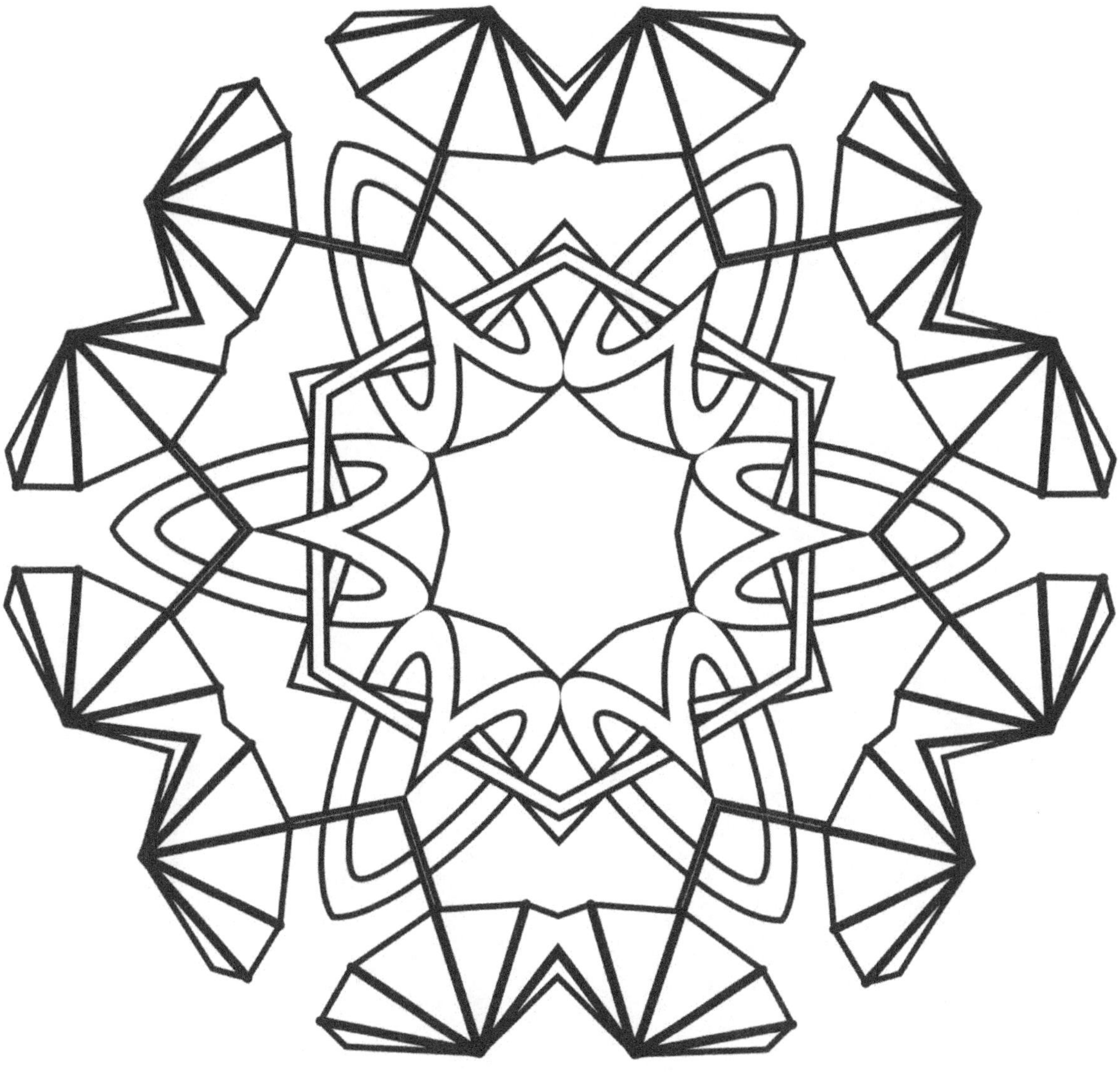

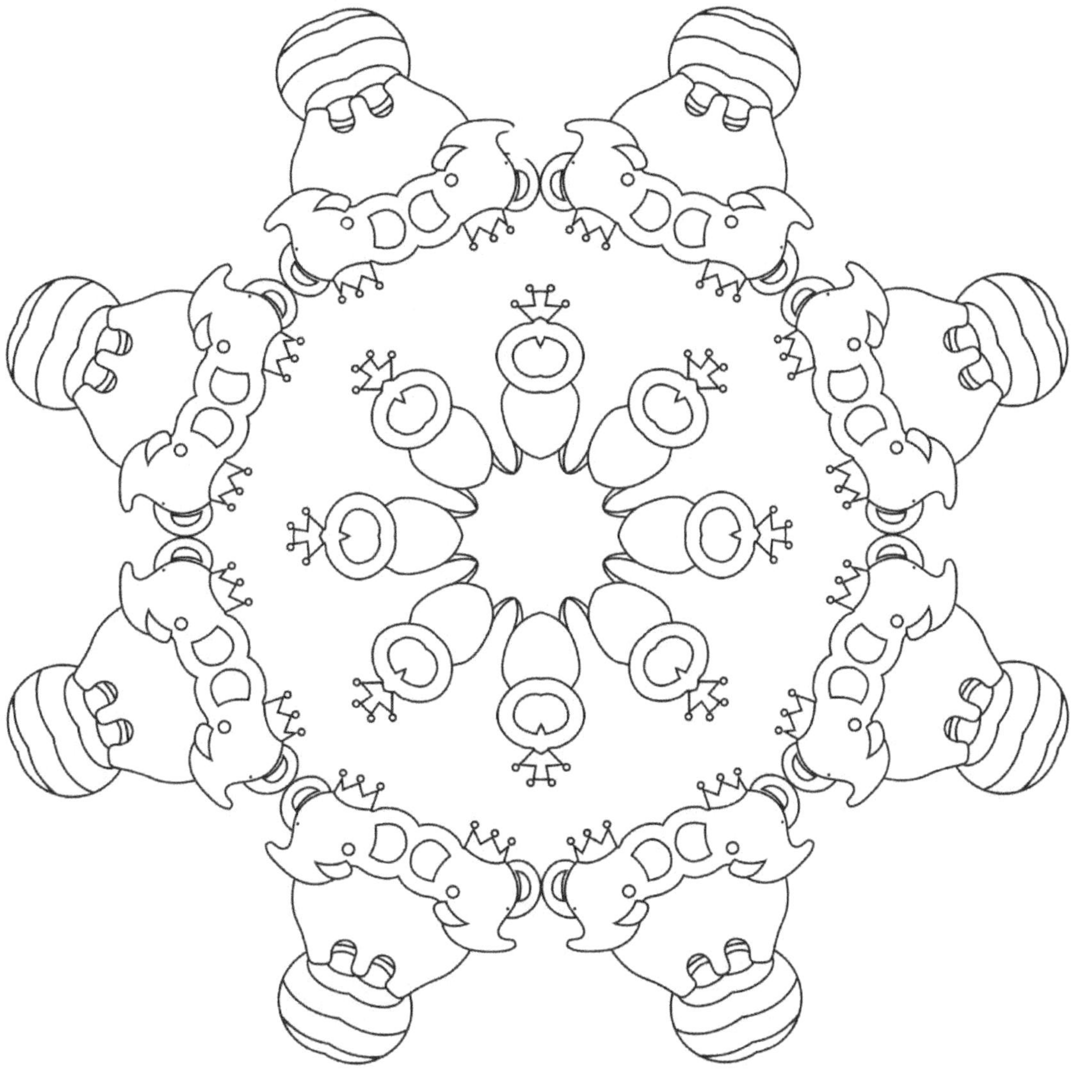

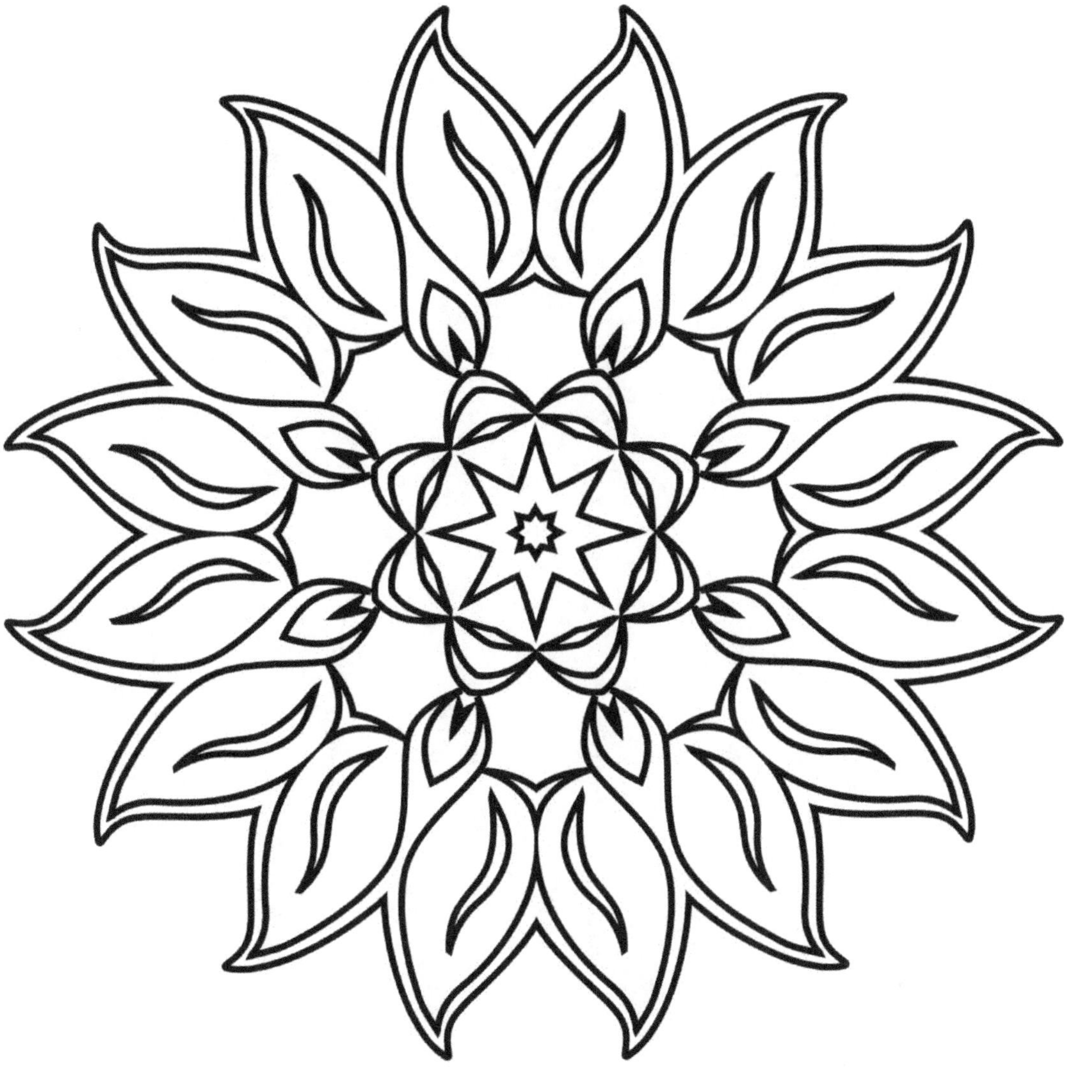

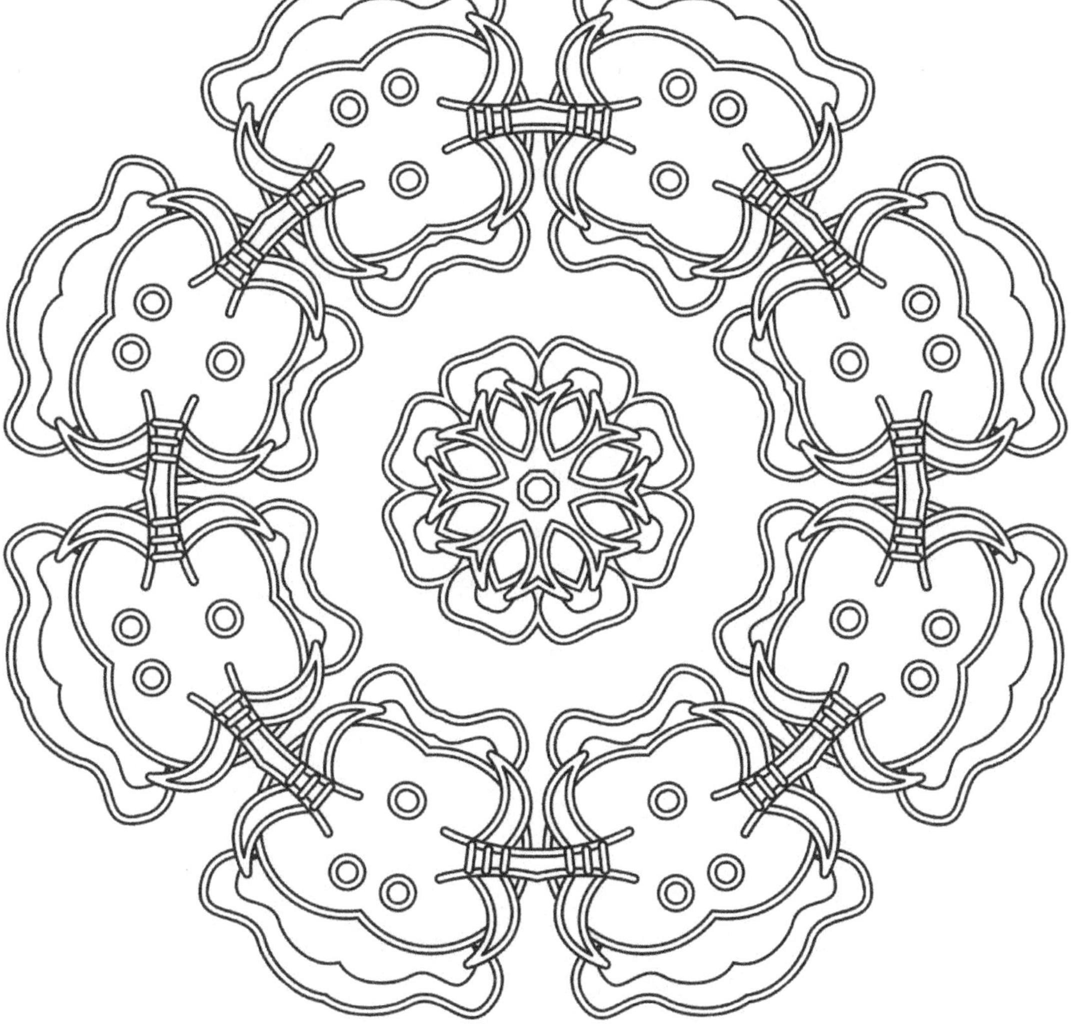

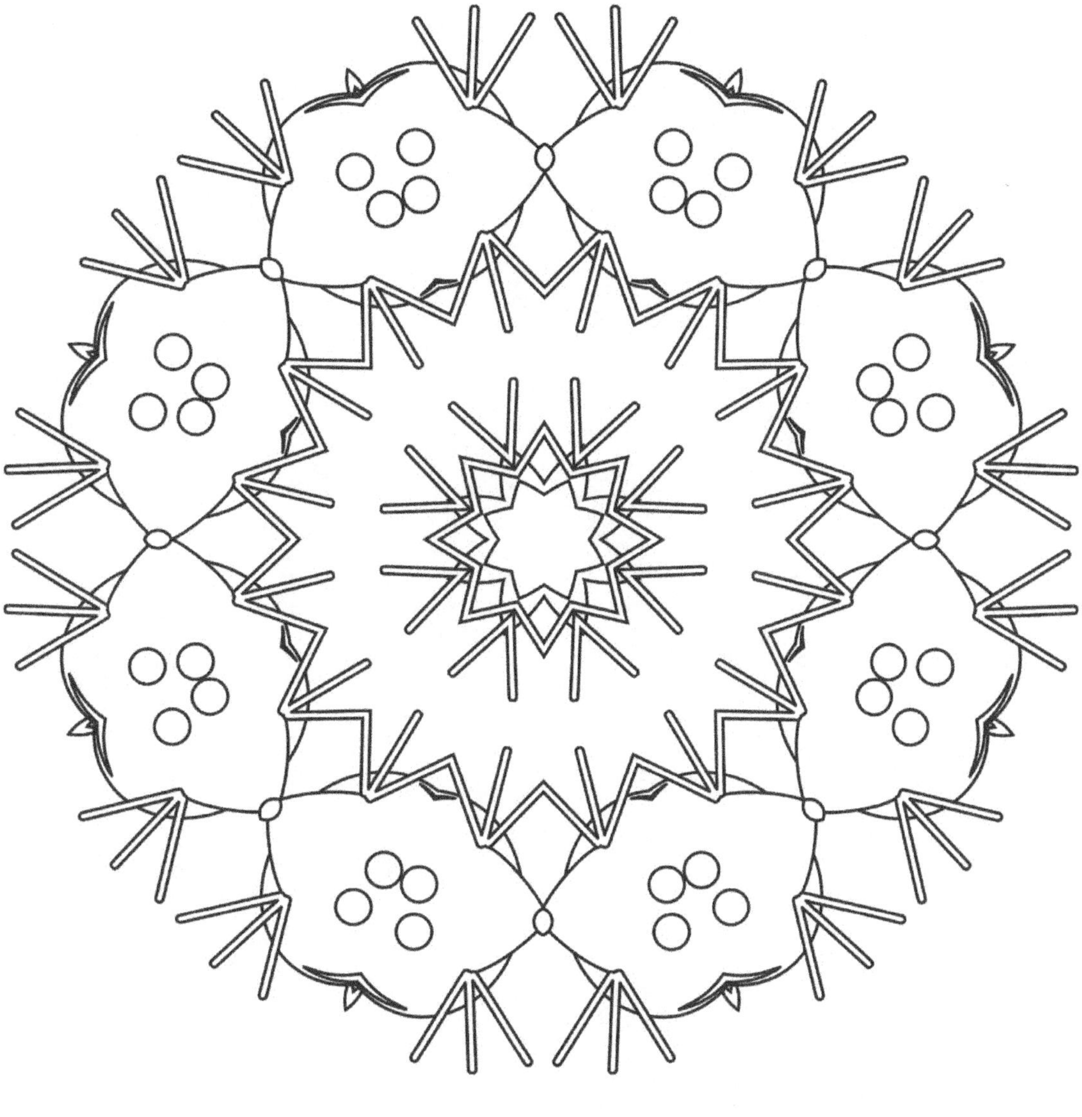

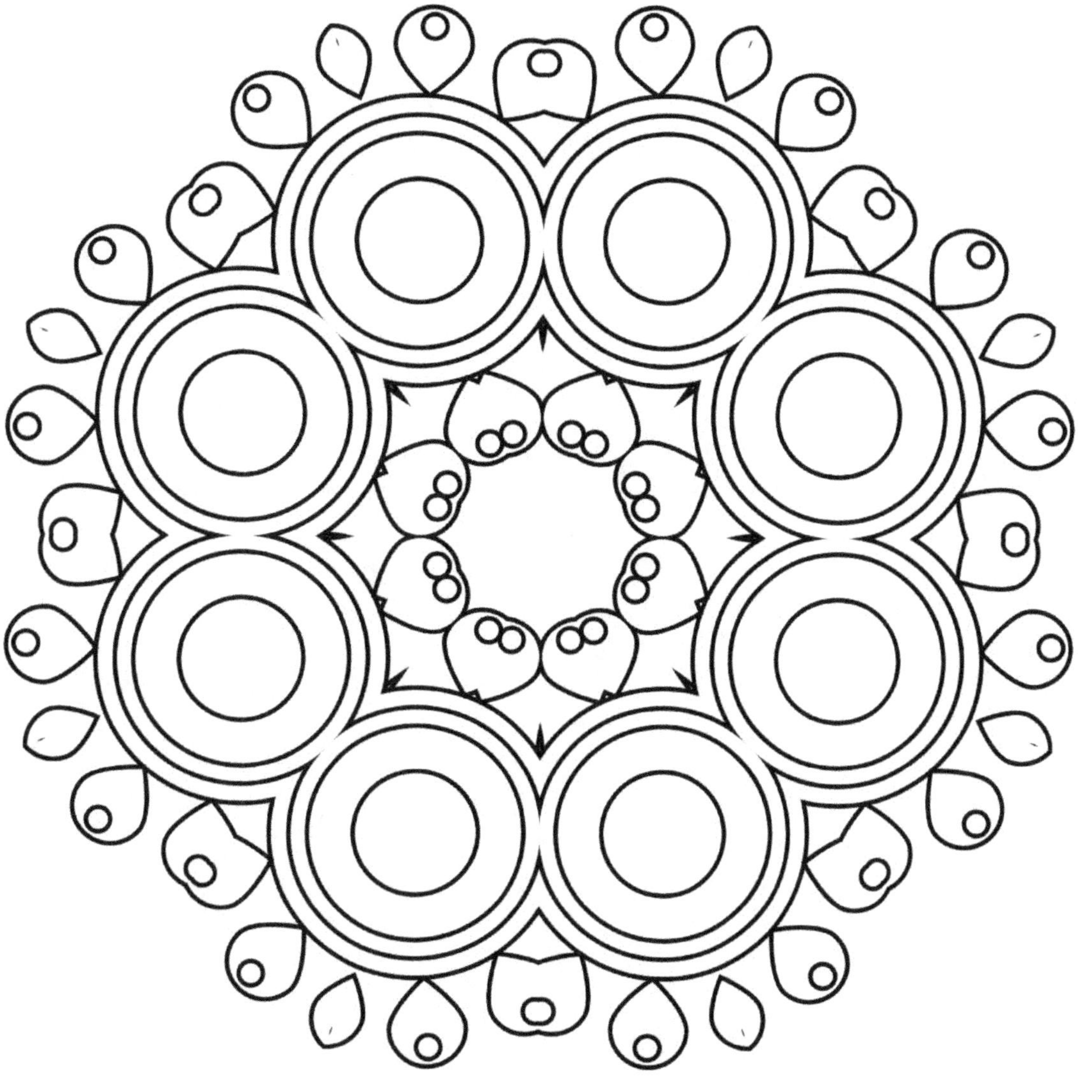

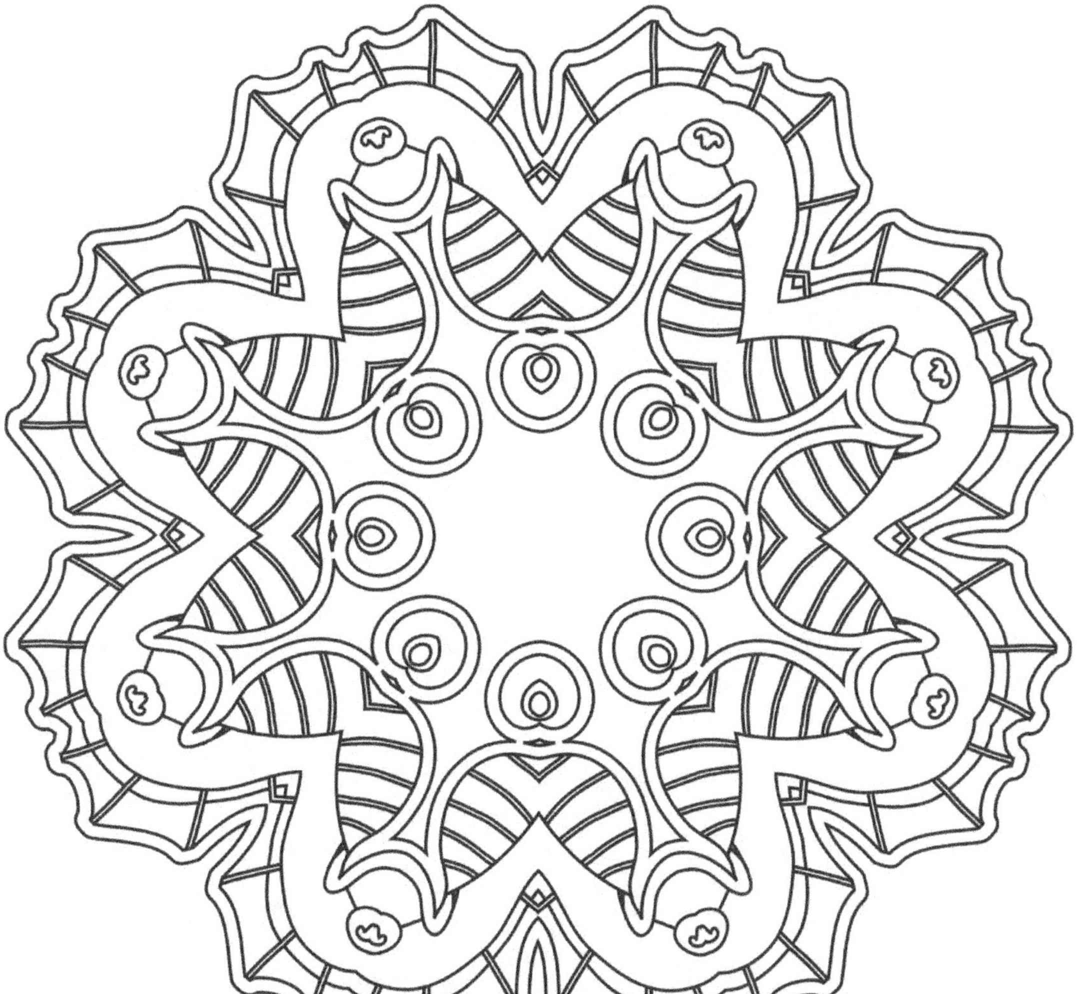

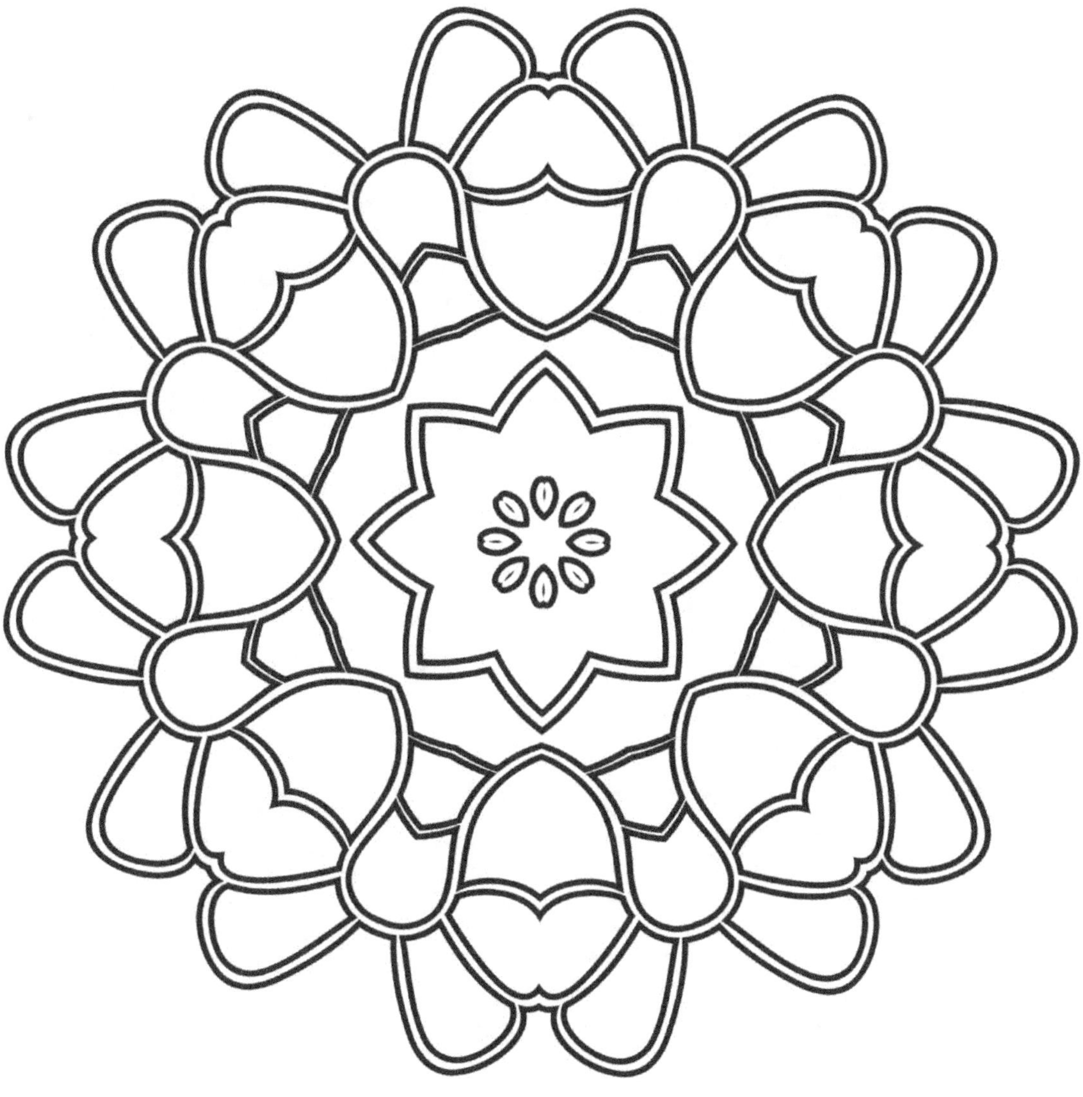

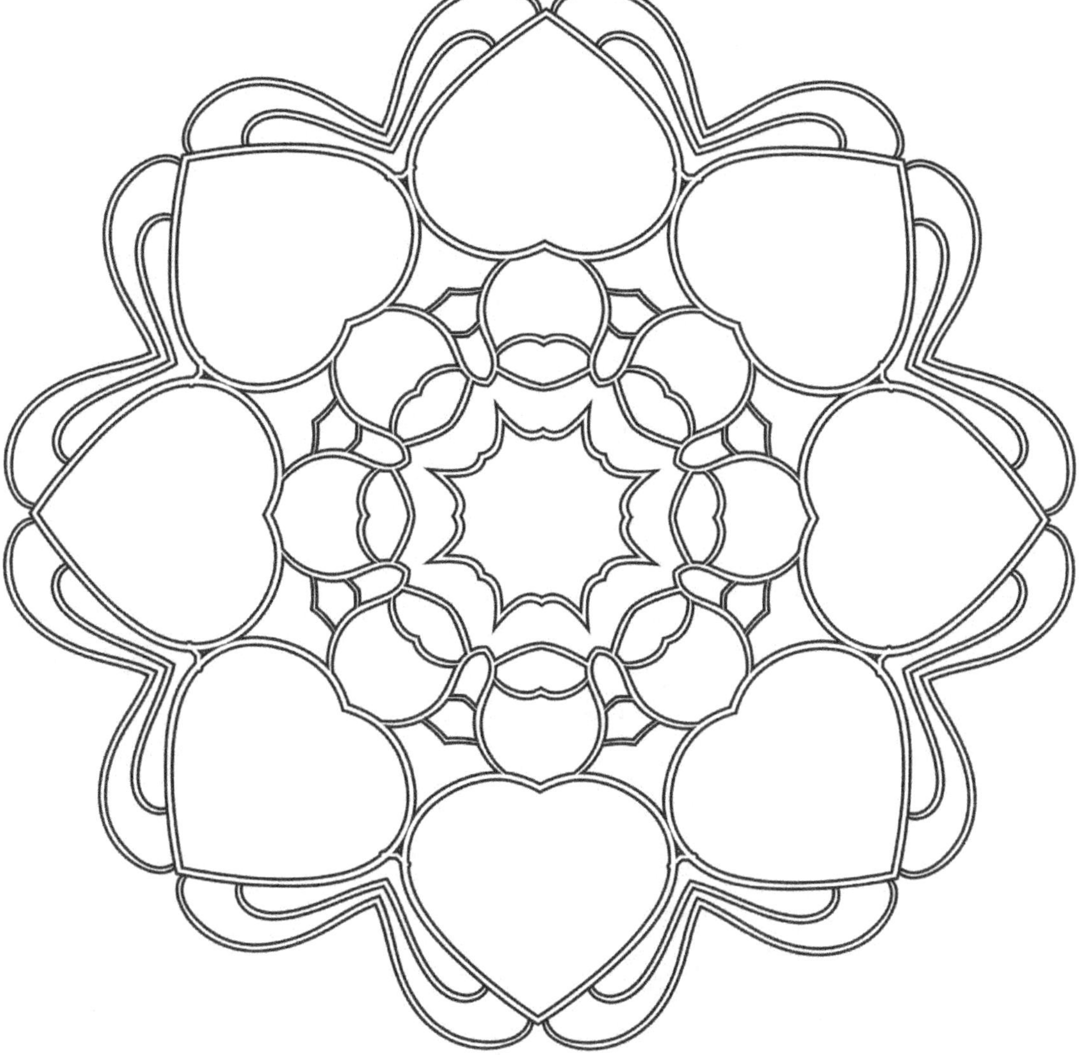

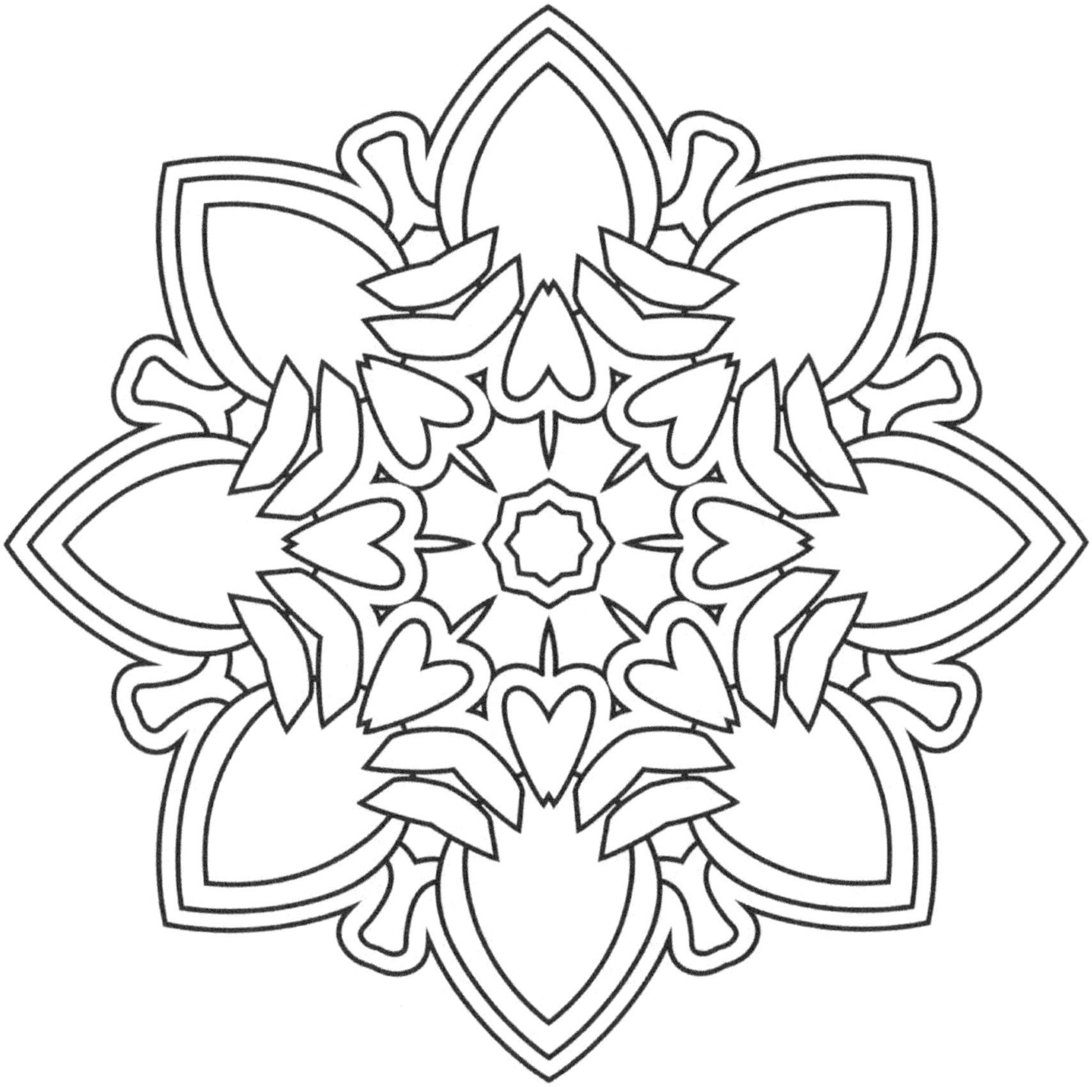

A Note About The Author

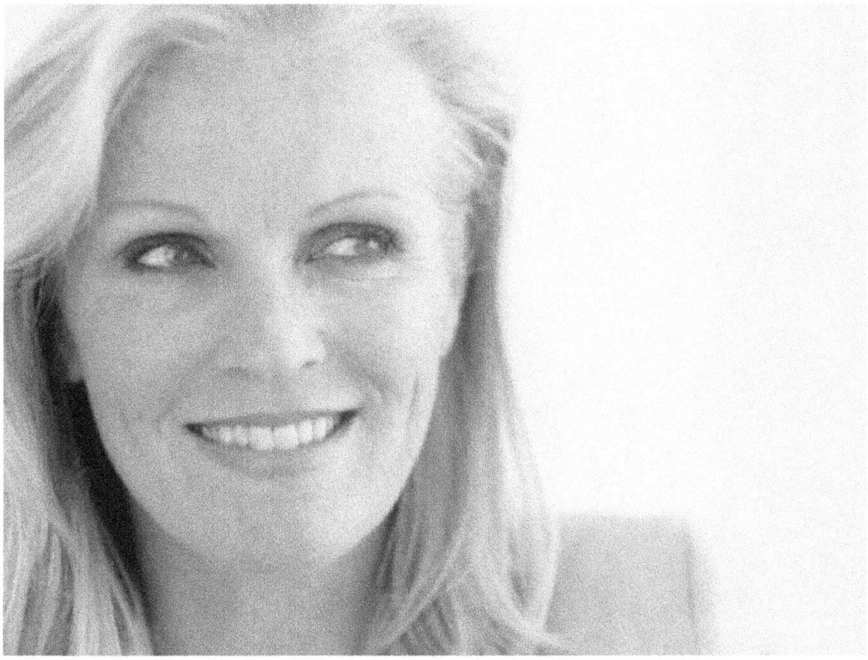

Belinda L. Frazier
Feel free to contact Belinda L. Frazier at belinda.coloring@gmail.com

Check out their Amazon profile here:

http://www.amazon.com/-/e/B01FSO94TA

www.ingramcontent.com/pod-product-compliance
Lightning Source LLC
Chambersburg PA
CBHW080633190526
45169CB00009B/3381
* 9 7 8 1 5 3 4 8 6 5 1 5 0 *